From The Heart

More Poetry by Brian Haydon

From the Heart
More Poetry by Brian Haydon
ISBN 978-1-923038-03-5
Copyright © Brian Haydon 2023
brian@haydons.com

A catalogue record for this
book is available from the
National Library of Australia

brianhaydonliterature.com

About the Author

Brian Haydon is a poet, playwright, musician and radio presenter.

In the first phase of his life he was a sportsman, with successes in swimming, Australian Football, track and field and rugby.

In the second phase he gained an honours degree in Industrial Engineering, a Ph.D. in Queueing Theory, and a Rugby Blue.

In the third phase he worked for a living, becoming a senior manager of Information Technology in International Airlines Qantas, Cathay Pacific and British Airways, and as a self-employed business consultant.

After 23 years living abroad, in Hong Kong and London, he returned to his roots in Australia for the fourth phase, dabbling in the performing arts, literature and volunteering.

Also by Brian Haydon

Out of My Head – Brian Haydon's Poetry

Brian Haydon Plays

A Tribute to Harry Bell

Stories of a Lifetime

3 O'Clock Thoughts

Introduction

This book had various potential titles – Tertiary Rhymes (v Nursery Rhymes), Thoughts and Fantasies, The Pleasure Spot, The Good Things in Life etc.
I learnt from my first poetry book that poetry doesn't sell, unless you are famous like Clive James or Les Murray, or in an anthology set for school curricula.

So why bother?

For some reason, e-books and paperbacks seem more desirable than scraps of paper and computer folders and files. That may sound selfish, but it works for friends and family too. These poems, written between 2021 and 2023, have never been published before. Here are 56 new poems to enjoy – one a day recommended.

I put together two books of poetry at about the same time. The contents are from the same period, but this one contains the positive thoughts, observations of nature, and passions. The other, titled "3 O'Clock Thoughts", is, as the name suggests, more philosophical, with issues viewed at a distance, or contemplated late at night.

Contents

About the Author 3

Also by Brian Haydon 4

Introduction 5

Contents 6

The Dancers 10

Love and Life of a Princess 12

Limerence 15

A Limerick on Limerence 16

Two-Timers – a Haiku Trilogy 17

Little Things 18

Momentary, Momentous Love 22

Passion 23

From Afar 24

Kindling 26

A Gold and Silver Pendant 27

Encouragement 28

Fantastic Dancing 29

Knights and Damsels 30

Fond Memories 33

Giftitude 34

Redwood Lovers 35

Consent 36

It Remains a Mystery 37

A Seventh Seven-Year Itch 38

At a Distance 39

Dreams 40

Bowral the Beautiful 41

Best Friends 42

Perfection 44

Rediscovering White 46

Shakespeare 47

Memories of Harry Bell 48

A Toast to Carers 50

The Humble Horse 52

Imagination 55

A Free Choice 56

Places 58

Shades of Green 60

Going to Sleep	62
Hope	64
Some Thoughts on Spirituality	65
Gratitude	66
Posthumous Orgasm	67
Something to Really Celebrate	68
Imagination v Memory	70
A Future Memory	72
Shade	74
Solutions	76
Nature at Work	77
Oh, Tree	78
Wilt	80
Nature's Music	82
The Blitz	84
Trees	85
Mice	86
Winter	87
Vax	87
A Haiku Treelogy	88

More Occupations 89

The Dancers

The party was raging,

cocktails galore

princes of the precinct

the beautiful people

and the dancers swayed in the middle

Stories were told

Laughter was heard

The days before selfies

The LaLa landers,

And dancers locked eyes

Sumptuous food,

exotic cocktails.

Fine wines

Silver service cutlery

And the dancers embraced

Corks popped

Champagne flowed

Flutes clinked

In toasts to each other

And the dancers kissed

Hours went by

The crowd thinned out

Lunches arranged

Thanks and appreciation

And the dancers kept kissing

Like the referee at a prize-fight,

the host tried to break the clinch

He needed a crowbar

Such was the tie

And the dancers separated

For fifty years.

Love and Life of a Princess

She the Hollywood beauty Queen,
Turning heads wherever she'd go,
Charming the punters, though not on the screen,
Saying "sorry, I'm taken" to each would-be beau.

She laughed at life and was quick with a smile
Dazzling her customers and inspiring their trips
She'd dress to kill and party in style
The life of the party, dishing out clever quips.

A brilliant photographer, and photographee
She dabbled in painting, she had a good eye,
She won many hearts, some from over the sea,
And set hearts a-flutter in many a guy.

In her long dress of satin, in emerald green,
She sparkled, among all the misses,
And made some male visitors terribly keen
imagining lingering kisses.

One begged her to take him somewhere to continue,
The fever had reached a high pitch;
She left him a-quiver in every sinew

Alone in his emotional ditch.

She married as planned and waved bye to the hills
To a strange place renowned for its pork;
Created a family and worked on her skills,
Rarely with old friends to talk.

Lost to the radar for many a year
Except for seasonal greetings
She published on Facebook her photos so clear
But not many physical meetings.

To the crossroads of the East, with its many connections
She settled in Georgian splendour
Where Ray Charles sang of his early rejections
And acceptance, with feelings so tender.

There she lived with the cards from fate she'd been dealt,
Like a card sharp dealing out magic;
Uncomplaining, as usual while inside she felt
Some of the cards turned out tragic.

A confident shell enclosed inner shyness

But her children ensured peace of mind
And very few knew that her thoughts in the night
Brought up aspects she'd like to rewind.

Half a century has passed since those Hollywood times;
Memories of dates need upgrading
Confused in life's disappointing nickels and dimes
Just time and age can cause fading.

We all should indulge ourselves, nostalgia rules
Dig out those moments to savour;
There may have been moments when we were but fools
But don't regret loving behaviour.

For love is a mystery, the greatest of feelings
It overwhelms logic and thought
And all through our history, in all of our dealings
Sometimes our love comes to nought.

So replay those moments, relive before sleep
Hope that you'll dream them once more
For they are real treasures, ones you must keep.
Keep them open - don't close the door.

Limerence

You've invaded my mind;
A friendly invasion, it must be said.
I left the door open, and there you were.

You've occupied every corner,
Every niche and every hollow;
Defences once shuttered have started to stir.

What to do when defences
Are overwhelmed, stormed?
Resistance is futile, go with the flow.

My memory cells are connected
To my smile muscle, so I grin;
And the reason no one will know.

30 May 2021

A Limerick on Limerence

To the city lights ever so glimerant

Came the bush poet ever itinerant

But just a slight shove

And a city gal's love

Turned him into a jelly-like limerent

1 Feb 2022

Two-Timers – a Haiku Trilogy

we are two-timers

someone is always asleep

except small windows

much calculation

of time zones and sleeping hours

just to have a word

there's so much to say

but no chance to say it

treasure each moment.

4 Feb 2022

Little Things

A sigh

a pout

a frown

a faint nod

a faint shake

a raised eyebrow

a sneer

a grimace

a glare

a wink

a triple-blink

a leering grin

eyes wide open

eyes squeezed shut

a sniff

a deep breath

a lip-lick

a growl

a nose twitch

a chin stroke

a hair pat

a murmur

a gasp

a giggle

a laugh

a bead of sweat

a smile

Little things mean a lot.

Temporaneousness

Joys of after-taste
Can a wine have a refrain?
Bliss on the palate.

Joys of after-glow
Basking in comfort and joy
Perhaps a replay?

A glorious act
A mere scintilla of life
Forgotten by most.

24 Sep 2022

Momentary, Momentous Love

It courses through you,
takes over your fragile brain,
swamping daily mundanities;
a flood of hormones
afloat, almost flying
afraid to touch
for fear of flickering sparks.
Engorged organs ache;
every sense heightened;
lost in the moment.

The moment passes, but the years roll on.
There are regrets:
failure to follow up;
failure to memorise every detail for future reference.
Fate rolls out a long carpet,
with a loop near the end

And what remains of the moment?
Two partial recollections, trying to reconcile?
A strong force of attraction, futile but fortunate?
It's too late to roll up the carpet.

Passion

Passion gets a mixed rating.
It is not just about sex,
where it represents vigour,
excitement, panting,
extravagant physical interaction,
ecstasy, release,
sundry sound effects,
subliminal splendour,
superluminal indulgence,
a brain swamped with emotion.

Passion can apply to any obsession
with a hobby, a job, an activity;
in moderation it brings creativity,
expertise, focus, joy, sharing.
In excess it can lead to folly,
neglect of duties, boring behaviour,
even danger.

A person without passion
is a plane without wings.

26 June 2022

From Afar

You sleep, I wake.
You wake, I sleep
Your thoughts, opaque
Mine clear, but so deep.
You seek the stimulus of coffee
I seek the comfort of warm milk
My work-ready denim jeans
Your nightwear soft, satiny silk

Your thoughts are sparked by last night's dreams
My thoughts are troubled by the day's reams
Of backlogs.
As you doze, you fill with romantic notions
As I rouse, I look for magic potions.
Thoughts of food and food for thought
What opposites the fates have wrought
Separation counted in hours and miles
Intimacy in words and smiles.

Swapping flattery and gags and such
That can't substitute for a glancing touch
Or better still an enveloping hug
In front of a fire, on a bearskin rug

But for now via computer ones and noughts

We can only send words and thoughts

Dreaming of more, we wish on a star.

The same one we both see,

But viewed from afar.

Kindling

You are the kindling for my passion

A mere thought sets it aflame

It builds not to an inferno

But to a warming blaze

Fed by thoughts and memories

Fueling perpetual motion

A swirling inextinguishable whirlwind

Contained by distance

My dread is that some day it will fade

into embers.

Let it burn.

27 June 2022

A Gold and Silver Pendant

Acquired in a trip of respite

Of tropical, sensual delight

Of company so much kinder

A guaranteed tension unwinder

Stars in the ascendant

A gold and silver pendant

A focus, hypnotic reminder

A treasured thought finder

The past, the present, the future

One memorable

One momentary

One mysterious.

Encouragement

Times can be tough

We're left feeling rough

When life throws a curve ball at speed

We forget how to soothe

To make life more smooth

While sharing a broken heart bleed .

But every hurt mends

when you're blessed with good friends

Restoring your faith in humanity

Just stay brave and strong,

and you can't go far wrong

And you'll overcome every insanity.

Nov 2022

Fantastic Dancing

Oh, to dance without reservation
To snuggle up and feel the softness of your skin
Perhaps to lightly stroke your arm
And entwine fingers deliciously

To move to the music
In unison
To feel the harmony resonate in our brains
To emanate warmth and love

I can smell you
I can hear your breathing
I can see your dilated pupils
I can feel tiny tremors from your heart

We move closer, humming the song
We step back to dissolve our eyes into one
It is impossible not to smile
Even to laugh in ecstasy

This is slow dancing, this is vertical love-making
This is virtual heaven
A shame it is all fantasy.

Knights and Damsels

I fancy myself as a knight,
In polished armor.
I am happy in lists, living by them.
Sometimes I tilt at windmills,
Like my friends who lean towards wind power.

Chivalry is my middle name
Well perhaps not quite yet.
My mother, the Lady Mary Green, trained me
To open car doors, wave through those of the other gender,
and even to walk on the splashes side of the sidewalk.

Some of my friends have bought lordships,
And in the days of cheques their wives
Had their ladyship pre-printed on their cheques.
Of course that was in England,
Where sycophancy is a national sport.

Knighthoods are dying out, as are knights
Dodgem cars and drag races can't match jousting
And boxing can't match swordplay.
Ladies are now known as "fans",
And they don't give their silk scarves to their heroes.

Oh to rescue a damsel in distress,

Or as my page suggests, a damsel in dis dress

It's a green dress

Backless

For Knights in white satin.

Fond Memories

heart in a puddle

And my mind in a muddle

All from a cuddle

But wait, I'm amiss

To ignore part of the bliss

A perfect sweet kiss

But I must confess

Wrapped in a soft satin dress

Was softness to press.

Giftitude

I am a gift to you, and you are a gift to me

It's easy to be a gift

All you have to do is care . . . really care.

To care you need to know and understand

And feed needs:

Need for appreciation,

Need for reminders of what a good person you are

Need for dreaming of what might have been,

And the best of what has been;

Needs for a chuckle,

Need for sympathy,

Need for love;

And a desire to unwrap,

To discard the superfluous layers,

And get to the core of being.

Thank you for your gift.

6 Dec 2021

Redwood Lovers

In a log cabin

Surrounded by giant trees

Log fire blaze crackling

Sipping a cocktail

After walk on forest trails

Smell of pine needles

Contented lovers

Long awaited privacy

We make love for hours

Sept 2022

Consent

Her eyes rolling uncontrollably,
Pupils dilated;
Her hand guides my hand;
Stroking, poking, stoking the fire.
Murmurs in my ear, humming, muttering.
Blowing, caressing, sucking
In air in gasps and giggles.
Bodies seeking to maximise contact area;
Limbs a writhing mass like a pit of vipers;
Cheeks flushed;
Hair standing on end;
Osculatory marathon, glossolalia.
Mutual forensic cutaneous examination;
Odours with beautiful past associations
Moisture accumulation;
Inhibitions and self-consciousness shed
Along with the crumpled multi-textured fabrics
Palpitations almost synchronised,
A brief "don't" and a "stop"
Then a rapid-fire "Don't stop, don't stop."

Is this consent?
31 August 2021

It Remains a Mystery

The magician's trade
Secrets, illusions
I watch a hundred times
But it remains a mystery.

A bright-eyed lass
An attraction defying logic
I admire from afar
So she remains a mystery

Is it an illusion?
How can she stand out
From the crowd.
It remains a mystery.

And after half a century passes by
The memory haunts me.
Until it's resolved
It remains a mystery.

A Seventh Seven-Year Itch

If you survive a seven-year itch and not fall in the ditch,
you can suffer a second, be absurd for a third,
keep score after four, still strive after five
find a fix after six; but seven?

If you make it to fifty, halfway to a ton, you surely should
pause for applause;
they say the nineties are nervous, like a tie-break six-all
service,
but during 49 years, you've woken up 17,897 times.
That's a lot of out-of-bed climbs.

So it seems quite obvious, in fact elementary
That without being questioned, you're inevitably destined
To transcend the 7th itch and attain a half-century.
Who'd have thought?

29 Sept 2022

At a Distance

So far away;
in time, in space, in feasibility.
Physically impossible,
psychologically more than probable;
in fact all-pervasive.

So the physical world must be dismissed,
ignored as inconsequential;
while imagination takes the lead,
emanating thoughts,
hoping the energy is transmitted.

Can love overcome the horizon?
The so-called tyranny of distance?
Turmoil, a tornado of thoughts;
surely it can escape the confines
of the cage of bones.

Dreams

We will walk slowly;
We will whisper what we wish,
what we wanted when.

A swinging cane chair
is OK for lone reading,
but only for one.

We will sway as one,
gently entwined on a swing,
in full harmony.

13 Nov 2021

Bowral the Beautiful

Bowral the beautiful, green and serene

With people and sights worth admiring

We all know, who make it our home

It's where smart people go

after re-tyring

18 Feb 2022

Best Friends

"Tell me about your best friend" she asked me.

I thought.

Do men have best friends?

I couldn't think of one.

I wondered whether it showed a weakness.

Self obsession?

Laziness?

Do I need a best friend?

What would they be like?

Perhaps a partner, with skills that I lack.

Perhaps a confidente; would that bring comfort?

Perhaps a polymath, to inspire and teach me

Or perhaps someone powerful, the head of the pack.

It's simpler with girlfriends,

A mutual attraction can grow

And develop

And deepen

And After years of mutual training

And earned trust

Can become an elegant sufficiency.

Of course, it's rare to have an all-purpose partner and lover

A spouse can be best friend, perhaps for life

Love is unlikely to last without change,

But the residual relationship can be very valuable for both.

A toast to best friends

And all friends.

December 2022

Perfection

She went to my school, from a very early age,
and as years went by we both turned the same page.
For a while she was plump, but always quite pretty,
Excelling in sport, and often quite witty.

Her body took shape, well proportioned but slender;
to my mind perfection for one of her gender;
with never words needed to communicate feelings,
we never got round to proposals and kneelings.

We just drifted together as friends knew we would.
In private we cuddled whenever we could.
As nature took course towards consummation
we built us a nest, with nice ornamentation.

Succession assured, we inspected the world,
learning together as the mysteries unfurled.
Doing good deeds for the less fortunate souls;
achieving, without setting, little life goals.

She wasn't a spendthrift, but had excellent taste,
and was never frustrated by the challenges we faced.
We weren't entirely like birds of a feather

Doing some things apart, and others together.

Never needing to tell each other little white lies,
we could solve any problem through each other's eyes,
for there through her pupils I sank many times
sometimes for forgiveness for silly little crimes.

A match made in heaven, some said of our contentment,
while others around us suffered mutual resentment;
so if the above seems like slight exaggeration
It's because most of it came from my imagination.

Rediscovering White

Little Lady looking lovely
Flanked by your pride and joy.

New circumstances, not unforeseen
New opportunities, not unknown
New realisations, not really surprising
New perspectives, not previously obvious;

But how can one train or prepare for emotions?
For grief, for relief, for friends, for affection?
For solitude in a house built for two
For precious relics and music and brew?

I know what you'll do, or hope that you will
You'll start a new phase, not yet over the hill,
And through all the challenges you'll resile
And in good times and not so good, wear that wonderful smile.

Feb 2023

Shakespeare

Willy wrote, and wrote and wrote.
He had to keep writing to earn a groat.
He acted, too, inside The Globe,
sometimes in trousers, sometimes in robe.

With sonnets sure to seduce the lasses,
comedies for the non-intellectual masses,
tragedies based on stories historical,
poems of power, oft allegorical,

warriors brave, and some demented,
words that previously had not been invented,
complexities the sapiosexuals adore,
colourful characters with charisma galore.

Satire and comedy, so clever, oft rhymeless,
despite Olde English, works so timeless.
Hamlet even invoked the spirit of Nero!
I think you can tell he's my literary hero.

27 Aug 2022

Memories of Harry Bell

They don't make 'em like Harry any more
And more is the pity.
He frequently filled his friends with awe
Oft with a well-chosen ditty.
It wasn't just memories and tales of yore
Of suburbs, outback and the city
But anecdotes fitting for fads and folklore
Wistful, wise or witty.

Everyone agrees that Harry was gentle
I never once heard him curse
A lover of mysteries and challenges mental
With never a need to be terse
I wished that his brain was available for rental
To access his knowledge and verse
Our hero worship was not incidental
His scope was somewhat diverse.

For some, to seek out a poem brings pressure,
And some of our efforts are lame
While Harry prodigiously recalled, at his leisure,
People and horses by name.
Charming, generous, an absolute treasure,

And Latin roots often he'd claim;

My esteem for him simply exceeds any measure

Our world will not be the same.

I will miss Harry, and I won't be alone.

A Toast to Carers

A toast to carers, everywhere - Your selflessness impresses;
your tolerance is tribute to your handling of stresses.
We who know not what it's like, such responsibility to bear,
can only partially appreciate the kindness that you share.

You manage to bring order to many mundane messes.
How we could cope with such daily demands are anybody's guesses.
The lottery of life leaves you caged, by your sense of duty,
But your courage and perseverance is itself a thing of beauty.

One day the cage will open, and offer you relief,
but not before the inevitability of sadness, loss and grief.
Then you'll look back upon this time with pride and satisfaction,
the challenges you overcame, digging deep for traction.

So more than a toast, we send you love, your kindliness has earned it.
When temptation to give in came round you resolutely spurned it.
You had a life before this, and you'll have a life hereafter

And may you be rewarded with happiness and laughter.

1 Feb 2022

The Humble Horse

When allowed to roam free,
They form gangs, and destroy and decivilize neighbourhoods.
Prized by poets, with their flowing manes;
Beautiful, but elusive, wild, and untamed.

When fenced in they are well-fed prisoners;
Some train every day, and compete for trophies,
Like human athletes, some are sprinters, some endurers of distance;
Some leap over hurdles, some strut with elegant finesse.

Only the winners get to breed, and retire to a grassy paddock.
The rest suffer the unkindest cut, as equine eunuchs.
A pretty little filly becomes an old grey mare.
A High-strutting pony is led head-down to the knackery;

And below the elite are the workers,
Once prized for towing, hoeing and sewing,
Rounding up cattle and helping herd sheep
They were skilled, responsive and well-maintained

Once they bore knights into battle, dragged cannon through mud,
Towed omnibuses and trams, or stagecoaches,
Pranced ahead of surreys, buggies broughams and barouches,
Sleighs and milk carts, they were valued back then.

Sure they polluted the atmosphere, or rather the road
Some thought that London would sink under accumulated dung,
But their fuel was inexpensive, they were sometimes self-driven
But not union protected, nor able to keep pace with automation

Do they jockey for position, to get the lightest rider?
Are they saddled with long days of boredom?
Do they long for a stable life?
Do they feel reigned in when hot to trot?

Do they really have such a shoe fettish?
Can they harness all their energy to race sulkies?

Do they get the bit between their teeth at the starting barrier?
Do they aspire to emulate Bucephalus or Incitatus?

How do they feel about the humans around them?
Do they care, as long as food is abundant and loads are light?
Do they realise how much their owners adore them?
That love saves them from extinction.
A toast to the humble horse.

4 Sept 2021

Imagination

Money is no longer an issue

my account overflows

I have freedom to do what I want

the diary is empty.

Friends are available

whenever I choose

I smile inwardly and outwardly

because love is in the air.

The Wallabies win every match;

politicians are polite in parliament;

artists and poets are appreciated;

cancer is cured and poverty prevented.

Humour has made a comeback;

wars are fought on chessboards and playing fields;

imagination becomes the drug of choice;

there is scope,

and perhaps hope.

August 2022

A Free Choice

Like a morning mist the moisture mills around me;

Focus is futile in this fecund fog.

Swirling, sweeping, sweltering slog,

obscuring the skillful scholarly scales

which weigh up wild wishes and wash away wails.

Clashes of clumsiness killing all clarity,

delivering ideas with indelible disparity;

removed are the ragged but robust rules

that hasten hypotheses to history's fools.

Milky maths models make massive modifications

to lemmas that lit up with long-lived elation.

Those theses though thoughtful and thorough, they thrive

but reliable answers rarely arrive.

Fantasy, fading, infuses the few

who believe that fate favours that fallacy, forty-two.

Yes, the solution evades me.

The dilemma enslaves me.

The options incite me.

Possibilities delight me.

Divisions, revisions, everything but decisions!

The quandary remains, as energy wanes;

I'm frozen in frustration . . .

For I was given a free choice

16 Oct 2021

Places

Places for sleeping
Soft for the rich, hard for the poor
Plush, daytime showroom
Or a blanket on the floor.

Places for working
Physical or mental
Either sweating in a mine
Or meditation transcendental

Places for playing
At a field or fast computer
Chasing balls or riding waves
Or loading a laser shooter

Places for loving
Nature or bedfellows
Hiking trails and scuba diving
Poets and storytellers

Times and places for life's delights
For putting us all through our paces
Even work can be fun if properly done

In all of life's pertinent places.

18 Feb 2022

Shades of Green

Pantone gave numbers to the many shades of green
Some added names, the prettiest we've seen
Like Pickle, Pistachio, parakeet and pine
Some based on foodstuffs on which we might dine
We see olives and juniper, avocado and pear
Basil and green tea and lime, though it's rare.
Places like Paris and Pakistan each give a name
And India and Russia, also make a claim.
Nature gives fern green, seaweed and moss
And without jade and celadon we'd be at a Loss
The Emerald Isle likes shamrock and Kelly Green
In England bottle green and harlequin are seen.
British Racing Green, like forest green suits Robin Hood,
Or Hunter or jungle green, or army if he could.
Myrtle's the colour of our proud baggy green
Caribbean and turquoise make a spectacular scene
Kaitoke is dark, and Chetwode very light
Jade, teal and laurel make everything bright
Dollar bill is a sage-like colour
Viridien is greyish, now we're getting duller
Shrek has his hue, he's never been pink,
And chartreuse is named after a rather sweet drink
Hooker's Green isn't to wear on the street;

I fear William Hooker never thought of that link.
Crocodile, sea foam and chlorophyll I missed
And Xmas green and slimy green should make every list
Each a different colour, with a story behind it,
And I meant to wear my camouflage shirt, but I just couldn't find it.

31 March 2022

Going to Sleep

All in order, Captain:

Ablutions complete.

Preparation for tomorrow – clothes prepared, checklist on table;

Alarm set.

Home security, heating and lights programmed;

Vehicles fueled

Larder stocked for breakfast;

Linen change schedule checked.

All in order, doctor:

Ablutions, medications;

Alcohol and eating completed hours ago;

My Screens shut down hours ago, but they still flicker in other rooms;

Argument with partner completed with a civilised ending,

A book of escapism imbibed;

sexual activity, if appropriate, completed.

Relaxation technique, from toes up, completed;

Meditation breathing initiated;

Dream plan in place;

Stressful concerns blacked out.

Now to sink through the layers until the subconscious takes over.

I wonder if dying peacefully is like this.

19 May 2021

Hope

Hope

Pray

Wish

Lament

Empathise

Commiserate

But DO SOMETHING

Blame

Resent

Dislike

Stress

Worry

Hate

But FORGIVE

18 March 2022

Some Thoughts on Spirituality

He was spirited out of the country
She gave a spirited performance
A popular song refers to "Spirit in the Sky" as a deity
Christianity's Holy Trinity includes a spirit
people claim to be spiritual but not religious
Spirits are more alcoholic than wine
A volunteer is told "That's the spirit"
the Spirit of Saint Louis carried Lindbergh to fame
a genre of music was once classified as "negro spirituals"
Not now.

Spirituality can be everything or nothing
perhaps it is imaginary like "the soul"

I like to think of it as the brother of love and imagination

14 Sept 2022

Gratitude

I am grateful for all the wonderful people in this world

And that they outnumber the fools, the fuddy-duddies,

the cruel, the crass, the sycophants, the selfish,

The wastrels, the wowsers,

The liars, the lazy, the greedy, the grumpy,

The arrogant, and the evil.

12 May 2022

Posthumous Orgasm

I don't care much – I'll have no ire

Whether remnants are consumed by maggots or fire

But while I'm warm, allow me one spasm

Please let me enjoy one last orgasm

For after brain death, says Mary Roach,

A TED presenter and orgasm coach,

Proper stimulation of a fresh cadaver

Brings one last gasp for a lifetime raver.

Jan 2022

Something to Really Celebrate

Whatever happened to courtesy?
Why is everybody so rude?
Why can't we calmly disagree
Without using language that's lewd?

If only we could listen to others' thoughts
Put ourselves into their shoes
Argue from logic, accept shades of grey
Recognize different views

But no, now we cancel, censor, deny
Refuse to accept that there could be two sides
Now we're dogmatic, simplistic and loud
Vitriolic and abusive when opinion collides.

Now we exaggerate, unsympathetically
Making it personal, calling out names
Paint opponents as evil,
Pouring fuel on the flames

My little appeal is for empathy,
Subtlety and balance a balm;
Listen, address the question;

Reply with wise balance and calm.

Our politicians could set a better example.
And we could celebrate our civilization.

3 Dec 2021

Imagination v Memory

There was a joust.

Both were confident.

Memory was adamant.

Imagination was skeptical.

In the early stages it was one-sided:

Memory reigned, undefeated;

Imagination was weak and underdeveloped.

Gradually, like a challenger usurping a champion,

Imagination took over;

richer, vibrant, accessible, pleasurable.

Meanwhile, Memory was fading;

Unreliable, dominated by favouritism,

Confused by competing priorities,

overwhelmed by new rivals.

New Memories also pushed Imagination aside.

The mental gymnasium was inadequate for both.

It needed a booking system – a schedule

for dedicated attention.

Imagination had its team of helpers:

visual art, psychedelia, relaxation, music.

Memory's team had photographs, histories, movies.

Mostly they went their own ways,

but occasionally a battle flared up,

With guest judges to make rulings.

Finally, Wisdom intervened,

and both admitted their weaknesses

and retired to pontificate,

neither influencing the world,

as the sun set slowly in the west.

25 Feb 2023

A Future Memory

It is 2026, I am 90.
I seem to be free of pain.
My muscles have regenerated;
my joints are supple;
my hair thick and dark;
my six-pack visible;
my skin flawless;
sight and hearing, are intact.
I need no pills,
I can sing with a rich voice,
my waterworks are functional,
my memory is perfect – long and short term.
Concentration comes easily;
no problem is too complex;
I can sculpt and paint with flare;
I churn out highly-acclaimed poems and songs daily;
my bookshelves contain my several best-sellers;
I have finally mastered sight-reading;
I play several instruments fluently;
I can break-dance,
somersault, high dive,
jog without a limp,
climb ladders safely.

Cheap, reliable power is available.

There is peace in our time.

As ever, my imagination knows no bounds.

25 Feb 2023

Shade

It was a miserable Summer in 2022-3.
It was as if Australia was infected by some climate pandemic imported from England.
Daily drizzle, grim greyness, permanent cloud cover.
Somewhere up there the sun was on an untimely vacation.
Meanwhile the swimming costumes were shrinking,

Then, in January, Summer stuttered back to life.
The sun emerged from its extended hibernation,
starting up in splutters, like a neglected petrol engine.
It fired up, and the new fire warning signs,
after a dose of WD40, moved their pointers from white to green.

The sky boasts a fresh gloss of blue;
the sparse clouds turning virgin white.
The grasses, illuminated by the powerful arc lights after months of drenching,
have now sprung to life in growth spurts;
but most of all, there are at last some shadows –
oases of shade, extra entities among the flora.

A landscape enriched by the juxtaposition of light and shade,
each shadow a sun-dial, slowly moving and growing until the sun exits stage West.
In this theatre of nature, the house lights fade up and the curtain closes on another day.
Welcome back, beautiful shade. See you tomorrow?

Brian Haydon, January 2023

Solutions

Solution to thirst
After days lost in desert
A glass of water;

Solution to stress
From fear, ambition, failure
Deep meditation;

Sad, sick and lonely?
Seek out company and share
Forgiveness and love.

1 Mar 2022

Nature at Work

bursting from a seed
intuitively driven
striving to expand

straining to surface
breaking through in full blossom
nature wins again

suck in CO_2
oxygenate the planet
Fabulous fauna

4 Jan 2022

Oh, Tree

Oh, tree!

What a life!

Honoured as a sapling, sprinkled with holy water

Seeking sunshine

Hungry for that "evil" CO2

To oxygenate our air, and shade our flowers

Welcoming koalas

With succulent leaves

Nests for birds, perches for parrots

You have turned the wind into a symphony

Swaying in concert with the strings

Shedding bark an elegant striptease,

revealing firm flesh

To later be renewed

Safe in suburbia

and national parks

Until the dreaded fire virus attacks

Spread your limbs, be a climbing frame

Your presence is comforting

Thank you, tree.

Nov 2022

Wilt

We came from seeds – you by chance, me by design
The early times were difficult – I had to be nurtured,
You had to wait for opportunities before appearing.
I was fed, sheltered, nourished;
You stayed in your shady spot and fed yourself;
I had a brother who grew tall and looks like living for a century.

You grew beside an oak, that sheltered you from the storms
We both had a prime – it will also live a century or more.
I saw how the bees adored you, but they kept away from me.
I saw how you blossomed and swayed to the rhythm of the wind
Like I moved to the music of my kind.

We were both handsomely straight of back.
Strangers admired us both.
The seasons were a delight for me, but for you they were disturbing
I was sad when I say your petals fading and leaves falling
My hair was falling out too, but it happened more gradually.
Then your back started bending.

Stooped, like the poor people in the nursing homes.

Your neighbouring oak was still a sapling, but he was as sad as me
I watched you shrivel up and shrink back to whence you came.
Ashes to ashes, dust to dust, they say.
I suppose I will eventually curl up and die.
I hope it is natural, like yours
And not by an implement seeking to hurry up renewal.

24 July 2021

Nature's Music

The wind rustling leaves
Swaying long grasses bowing each other
Pizzicato rabbit chatter
Nature's String section

Then howling across the hills
Silent until it encounters something to vibrate
Whistling through the hills
Nature's brass section

Rain's Pitter patter on the rocks
Disturbing the possums and cockatoos
Branches clattering to the ground
A percussion section.

cockatoos call and respond
Galahs play trios in harmony
The kookaburra chorus swells and subsides
Vocalists of the bush

Torrents pound the rocks
Hissing a spray and spurting spumes of foam
Breaking away banks

Nature's water music.

After the crescendo, a lull.
John Cage's silence is music to the ears
After the storm subsides, it's still and silent.
But it's just an interval in nature's symphony.

Jan 2022

The Blitz

The colony is in quiet uproar

Alarm bells are ringing silently;

Chemical warfare , the dreaded white powder,

Seeping down into the tunnels.

The wounded desperately limp to safety.

Keep calm!

Wait for the bombing to stop.

Protect the children;

Protect the children to be.

Assemble the troops.

Those who peeped outside see devastation;

White powder everywhere.

Soldiers trying to shake off white powder from their backs

The bomber casting a shadow over the grand entrance.

Scouts reporting in and then collapsing.

The bomber departing.

He wins the battle, but not the war.

It is not the first bombardment of a nest

By ant powder.

Nor will it be the last.

12 April 2021

Trees

Trees

Dancing in the brutal wind

Please

stop dropping leaves and bark

And branches

Stop undressing in front of me.

And those denuded branches

Are not attractive.

A little makeup

In the form of leaves

Would improve your appearance.

But fear not. I still love you all

And the kin that surround you.

Your beautiful families

Even if they can't sway in time with each other.

15 Feb 2020

Mice

Little furry mice

Leaving a trail of faeces

Destructive critters

Pantry explorers

Ripping apart packages

Devouring powders

Eat peanut butter

Served up on a trap platter

Or I'll buy a cat.

Sept 2022

Winter

It's nearly Winter

The aches and pains reappear

Time for some hot soup.

Vax

A pin-prick today

Fights disaster tomorrow

Best be "we" not "me".

A Haiku Treelogy

Treebute

you sway and flutter

flex as you dance with the wind

limbs longer each year

Treebulations

Shed leaves like dandruff

Blot out the nourishing sun

Bark in twisted strips

Obitreeary

and when you grow old

you grow stiff, wither and die

replaced by saplings

31 May 2022

More Occupations

I'm a hand therapist, I stroke fingers all day
I sew slings and stretchers and hope that they stay
I provide heated towels, and hot wax rinses
I squeeze and stretch sinews, watching eyes for winces
My clients go home happy, with games they can play,
With rubber balls to knead, and playdough-like clay.

Hear my beeps, till your limits are nearing
I play you sounds beyond human hearing
I speak very softly, and tell you it's clear
That you need some assistance to be able to hear
For I'm an audiologist, I confirm what your spouse
Has been saying when you thought they were quiet as a mouse.

Many more occupations are covered in "Out of My Head – Brian Haydon's Poetry". There will be more in the future; for instance a dental examination is imminent, and several specialists.

www.ingramcontent.com/pod-product-compliance
Lightning Source LLC
Chambersburg PA
CBHW071322040426
42444CB00009B/2066